Just Because You Can Cut Your Own Hair Doesn't Mean You Should

Humorous Observations on
Why Marketing Is Best Left to Professionals
and Helpful Tips Should You Decide to Go It Alone

Roger D. Hicks

Just Because You Can Cut Your Own Hair Doesn't Mean You Should

Humorous Observations on Why Marketing Is Best Left to Professionals and Helpful Tips Should You Decide to Go It Alone

ISBN 978-0-578-60666-8
Printed in the United States of America

Some characters and events in this book are fictitious. Any similarity to real persons, living or dead, is a coincidental and not intended by the author.

Editing by Electrum Branding
Front cover image by Thomas LaBadia
Book design by Electrum Branding

Published by Electrum Branding

www.RogerDHicks.com

This book is dedicated to my parents who inspired me to learn,
Ellen who taught me so much, and my clients
who gave me the opportunity to teach.

TABLE OF CONTENTS

FOREWORD

When a classically trained chef is subjected to working in a grade school cafeteria or an artist makes his or her living painting houses, you may get an occasional tater tot flambé or an unsolicited mural – but the end result is likely to be frustration and despair. The same can be said of writers.

When creative writer Roger Hicks found himself at Electrum Branding, a boutique agency catering to a clientele comprised mainly of banks, accountants, wealth advisors and lawyers, he found that he had to shelve his conversational, humorous writing style for emotionless, informative corporate communication.

As he adapted his copywriting style to meet the needs of Electrum's clients, he kept mental notes of his interactions with them, prospective clients, vendors, and members of the Electrum team. As Roger became versed in inbound marketing, his mental library of content grew even larger. So when Electrum updated its website to include a blog as a way to establish itself as an authority in all things branding, Roger was off to the races.

Over the years, his blogs have covered a broad range of branding and marketing topics. But, whatever the subject, the content is always brief, informative, easy-to-read, often times humorous – but always entertaining. Roger's writing has become an integral part of the Electrum Brand and I invite you to read for yourself.

- Ellen Schlafer – Founder of Electrum Branding

INTRODUCTION

When Electrum Branding opened for business in 2004, there were no iPhones, Twitter handles, or YouTube videos (gasp). Facebook was still "The Facebook" and people sent emails to AOL accounts via their BlackBerrys. And, most websites were clunky electronic brochures that didn't display well on tablets, because well, there were no tablets.

Despite opening during what we would now consider the dark ages, the Electrum team managed to successfully build our customers' brands and position them to find, get and keep customers. We've learned a lot over the years. As technology advanced, learning was mandatory.

But most of what we learned came as a result of measuring results, following best practices, and keeping an open mind. And now, we'd like to share with you the top marketing tips every business owner should know in order to grow their business.

CHAPTER 1

Write for Your Audience, Not Your CEO

At Electrum Branding, we excel at crafting brand messaging for our clients that effectively conveys the value proposition their customers can expect and enjoy. For some, it's a memorable dining experience — for others, exceptional customer service, unparalleled industry knowledge, or a cutting-edge solution to an age-old problem.

Although we have clients with easy-to-market attributes, leading them to a simple brand message is not always easy. As the saying goes, you can lead a horse to water, but you can't make him tell you why in 10 words or less.

What the Spec?

Some clients are so proud of their products' technical capabilities that they confuse a laundry list of product specifications with actual benefits. It is then our job to find the benefits in the list – much like Dian Fossey looking for a remote pack of primates. We study the product in action, find the lead silverback, I mean benefit, and build our message around that.

Maybe the Lingo Ate Your Baby

Then there are clients so entrenched within their industry that they assume everyone understands their jargon. WRONG! SEO, APY, RDC, API, and LTV are not benefits, they're abbreviations. Your brand message should be written for your consumers and not for your colleagues.

There is no U in Benefit

Some clients have a very rich history of success. That's great; however, content should not be about you, your business or your industry. It should be about your customers, their lifestyles and their aspirations – how you make their life better, play a vital role in their lifestyle, and help them reach their goals.

Passion Brut

The Passion Brut is so convinced that his or her product is so spectacular, it's assumed that everyone else is equally zealous and clamoring to know more. And why wouldn't they? It's a robe AND a blanket! Seriously, while we dream of one day landing the Snuggie account, we always recommend that "creating interest" precede "conveying information."

A few rules to follow:

- Use simple honest language that creates interest, not information overload
- Write to impress your consumer and not your CEO
- Replace confusing jargon with clear benefits
- And, inform your customers how your product will make their lives infinitely better.

Adhere to these guidelines and you'll create a brand message that will resonate with your audience and motivate them to take the desired action.

CHAPTER 2

Facts Tell. Stories Sell.

Facts tell. Stories sell. Keep this in mind when you're marketing your brand. How well do you tell your brand story? Are you honest yet engaging? Do your descriptions leave nothing to the imagination? And above all, are you brief? Need help telling your brand's story? Just look to master storytellers past and present for tips on how to create a brand story that will engage your audience.

Wow Them Like Walt

Walt Disney knew that subtlety and storytelling did not mix. So, follow his lead and fill your story with grandiose (yet honest) details about how your service or product will wondrously change your customer's life for the better. Giving a half-hearted description of your product is the equivalent of Cinderella wearing Crocs to the ball.

Be Personal Like Ellen

Ellen DeGeneres has a gift for drawing people into

her world and making them smile. You can too, if you: remember to not take yourself too seriously; don't be afraid to be funny; and, above all, make sure your audience is comfortable. Don't intimidate them by implying they are un-informed, poorly prepared, or unhip if they aren't aware of your product or service.

The Dickens You Say

Charles Dickens was a great novelist because his stories contain such vivid descriptions. We know exactly what Miss Havisham's sitting room looked like and can practically feel the fur-trimmed robe of the Ghost of Christmas Present. When speaking about your product or service, be vivid and colorful. Leave nothing to your prospect's imagination.

However, be aware that not all famous storytellers are cut out for the branding game.

Don't Be So Grimm

Masters of the folk tale, the Brothers Grimm were known for their tales of cruelty and violence – many of which have been sanitized for the movies. Spare your audience the negative details of your bad split with a former business partner, how the economy drove you into your line of work, or the challenges you face. Be positive and focus on the benefits your customers appreciate.

Leave Homer at Home

You may have heard of Homer's epic poem The Odyssey, but have you read it? (Cue the crickets.) I thought not. I am not saying there's anything wrong with a 12,000-line dactylic hexameter poem, but in branding, less is more – way more. Yes, be descriptive, be colorful, be grandiose – but also be brief. People have work, families, social commitments, and now six o'clock hot Bikram yoga – so let 'em have your brand story, but make it quick.

To Be or Not to Be Understood

Poor Shakespeare often gets a bad rap for being difficult to read. It's not his fault that people no longer use the same lexicon as they did then, or that we prefer our syntax un-inverted. Be sure to set your brand story in the present or, better yet, in the future being enjoyed by your target audience. Use words from their vocabulary and not from your product's technical manual.

Ready to turn your brand story into a best seller? Follow these messaging tips and you'll be on your way.

- Create an experience for your customers
- Provide compelling descriptions of your products' benefits
- Be descriptive about how your products or services will improve their life
- Use their lingo and avoid your jargon

- Avoid the negative and focus on the positive
- Be brief
- Share where your brand came from and how it came into existence

CHAPTER 3

Customer Experience Is King

If you've put more effort into getting customers in the door than providing them with a positive experience once they do, your business is doomed. This is something my husband and I learned firsthand after visiting a well-branded, yet poorly prepared, and now shuttered sandwich shop. Although this experience occurred in a restaurant, the lessons learned could apply to any business.

After reading several articles about a New York-style sandwich shop that recently opened in our neighborhood, we decided to support a local business and give them a try. Having dined at several newly opened restaurants, we anticipated a few hiccups in the service, but nothing could have prepared us for the comedy of errors that awaited us.

You Never Get a Second Chance to Make a First Impression

My husband and I were greeted by an eager hostess who invited us to sit anywhere we wanted, but then blocked us from moving forward and motioned for us to sit at the table immediately inside the door. Despite most of the tables being vacant, we obediently took our assigned seats. Our server, who I will call Trixie since she never offered her name, scurried off to get our drinks and returned quickly with two large tumblers half filled with soda.

Know Your Product

After several failed attempts to explain the difference between a turkey club and a turkey sandwich, Trixie became flustered and went to the kitchen to retrieve the cook. He was also stymied by the query and shouted for the owner to join in their tableside debate on the condiment content of each sandwich. And, although unintentional, they brilliantly formed a ring around our table which prevented our escape.

Back Up Your Claim

With his confidence now shaken, my husband decided to play it safe and order a turkey sandwich with cheese. When asked what kind of cheese they had, she replied "all the cheeses" but could only name American. In hindsight, I wish I had spent less time contemplating the vast storage space required to hold "all the cheeses" and more time requesting a specialty cheese. If the ingredients of a turkey club stumped poor Trixie, requesting a gently smoked Camembert or an aged Gorgonzola Piccante might have caused her to spontaneously combust.

Pay Attention to Detail

My husband eventually ordered a turkey sandwich with only provolone cheese and chipotle mayonnaise. So, imagine our surprise when he received a sandwich with turkey, bacon and no cheese at all – thus keeping their inventory of "all the cheeses" perfectly intact.

The Customer Is Always Right

When we pointed out that his sandwich was missing cheese but included bacon, which he did not order, Trixie suggested that he look under the turkey for the cheese and said she would not charge him for the bacon. Upon proving his sandwich was indeed cheese-free, she apologized and returned the sandwich to the kitchen for a makeover.

Be Empathetic

When the owner came by to see how everything was, my husband explained that his sandwich order was wrong, but Trixie was happily remedying the error. Rather than apologize, offer a discount or a coupon for a future visit, he turned and marched into the kitchen – apparently to reprimand someone – leaving us in awkward silence. *Did we just get someone fired?*

There's a Time and Place for Feedback

After his sandwich was corrected, we enjoyed a rather delicious meal. After eating our fill, we requested to-go containers. However, before bringing them, Trixie leaned on our table and began to interrogate us on what they could do better. Did the food taste good? Were the sandwiches too large? Did it take too long? Are the prices reasonable? Being in the customer experience measurement business, I am a huge proponent of customer feedback, but not delivered in this fashion. You grill the sandwiches, not the customers.

Build It Before You Brand It

As she handed over the to-go containers, I noticed they were branded with the restaurant's logo – as were the cups, the paper napkins, and the large rugs inside the door. As I looked around, it was easier to list the items not branded with the logo. It became apparent that the business owner had invested more in marketing (public relations, roadside banners, logo-branded everything) and less on training (product knowledge, product quality, customer service, problem resolution, and customer feedback).

Like many business owners, he focused on getting people in the door with little regard to the experience he would offer his customers – missing a powerful marketing opportunity.

If we had enjoyed a positive experience, we would have raved about it to our friends and posted to social media. But instead, I am writing this cautionary tale, wondering about Trixie and the current whereabouts of all the cheeses.

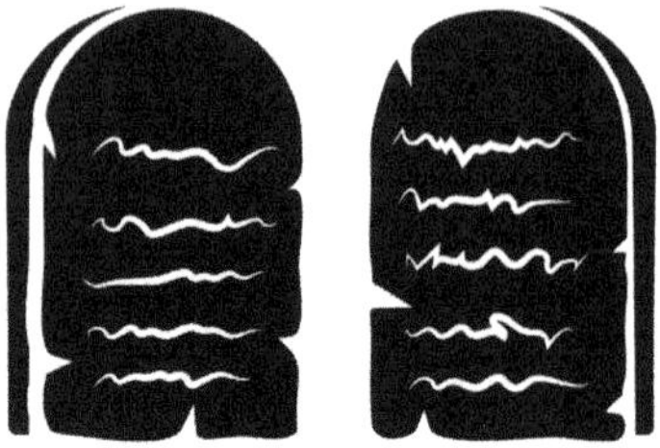

CHAPTER 4

The 10 Social Media Commandments

According to a recent Pew Research report, 65% of adults now use social media – an increase of more than 800% since 2005. Although it's clear that social media isn't going anywhere, many businesses continue to underestimate its influence on how we obtain information, how we make purchase decisions and how eager we are to share our experiences and influence others.

The good news for small businesses is that social media costs them just as much as it does a worldwide brand - absolutely nothing. Coca-Cola's Facebook page is not afforded any more bells or whistles than Homer's Hometown Honey. I'm not saying that Homer will find it easy to secure 107 million followers, but who knows. I doubt that Atlanta pharmacist John Pemberton thought his fountain-drink concoction would become a worldwide iconic brand.

The bad news for some businesses is that because having a social media presence is free, they don't treat it as a priority. Instead, they focus their efforts on items with a price tag attached – marketing, inventory, and payroll –

neglecting their social media pages and possibly damaging their brands.

I. Thou shalt not have a blank cover image.

Unless you're The Beatles and your content is as brilliant as The White Album, you need a cover image. The cover or header image spans your company page and should reflect your brand. The size of the cover image varies by platform, so follow these social media cover image guidelines:

Facebook:	820 pixels x 312 pixels
Twitter:	1,500 pixels x 500 pixels
LinkedIn:	1,584 pixels x 396 pixels

II. Thy logo must fit the profile image.

You wouldn't make your personal profile image a photo of your nose and a portion of your left eye. So why would you upload a poorly sized logo that doesn't display properly? Your profile image not only helps identify your page, but it also identifies your comments and posts to other sites so follow these social media profile image guidelines:

Facebook:	360 pixels x 360 pixels
Twitter:	400 pixels x 400 pixels
LinkedIn:	400 pixels x400 pixel
Instagram:	180 pixels x 180 pixels

III. Thou shalt not make it all about you.

Although individuals may use social media to post duck-face selfies, wish mere acquaintances happy birthday and find out what their goblin, pilgrim or elf name would be, a business should not be so self-absorbed. Eighty percent of your content should be non-promotional and be interesting or of value to your audience such as industry-related blog posts and articles. Even your promotional posts should focus on the benefits your audience can expect by using your product or service.

IV. Thou shalt not be anti-social.

You wouldn't have a party and not invite anyone so why bother setting up a social media page and not ask people to follow you? Unless you plan to throw a lousy party or have a horrific social media page, invite your employees, friends, family, vendors, clients, prospects, and referral sources to follow you.

V. Thou shalt not put thy head in the sand.

Just like in business, you should know what your competition is doing. Your competition may be a great resource for content ideas, but don't copy what they are doing – improve upon it.

VI. Thou shalt post regularly.

Would you shop in a store whose display windows

were empty except for a dusty one-armed mannequin lying on its side? Probably not. But that's the image you are projecting when you set up a Facebook page and never post any updates – uninviting.

VII. Thou shalt engage with thy audience.

If someone takes the time to post a comment to your page, the least you can do is "like" it. It may only take a second, but it shows your followers that you are aware and appreciate them. If a comment happens to be constructive criticism, welcome their feedback and use this open forum to show that you are listening and interested in improving. If a negative comment is offensive, remove it and offer to address their concern offline, while being sure to provide your contact information.

VIII. Thou shalt tag generously.

If you mention another business or follower in your post, do them a favor and tag them. Simply add an @ before their name for the link to their profile or page to appear. Note: You may have to create the post and then edit it after it is posted for this method to work.

IX. Thou shalt share.

No one is expected to come up with original content all the time. Look to your peers and industry thought leaders for shareable content. It not only gives you a day off, but shows your followers that you are up to date on industry trends and news.

X. Thou shalt not work independently of marketing.

Make that H.R., community relations and sales, too. Social media is a resource for all departments. Post about career opportunities, new hires and internal promotions. Promote events you are sponsoring or hosting. Post about upcoming sales promotions.

So don't let our mission to the social media mountain top have been in vain. Take these commandments and allow them to lead you into the social media promised land of "Likes" and money.

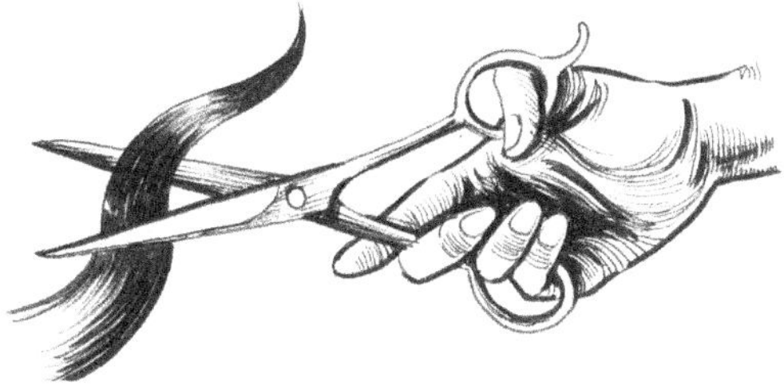

CHAPTER 5

Just Because You Can Cut Your Own Hair Doesn't Mean You Should

The same goes for marketing, yet people try it anyway. Marketing is like art. Not everyone can explain why it works, but they all know what they like. They chuckle when they recall, "Where's the Beef?" they can still sing along to "I'm a Pepper" and point and yell out, "Spuds Mackenzie!" when they see a bull terrier – even when it's Bullseye the Target dog.

Yes, I know, my '80s are showing and if you're younger than 35, I've probably lost your attention to something on Snapchat, TikTok or Twitter. But, for those of you still reading, my question is this: *When it comes to marketing, does clever, memorable or funny even matter if it doesn't get results?*

Beyond debating the merits of marketing being funny versus being memorable, there are many avenues you will need to navigate effectively in order to avoid the following pitfalls:

Premature Advertising: Spending money on getting the word out before deciding what the word should be.

What is your competitive advantage? How should it be communicated and delivered to your customer for optimum response?

Door over Floor: Focusing your marketing efforts on getting people in the door without giving any thought into what to do with them once they're on your sales floor.

You can never recover from a mediocre first impression. Have your people been adequately trained to present your products' benefits rather than recite lists of product specs? Can they upsell? Cross sell? What are your service standards? What is expected of them?

Myopic Selling: Focusing so much on products and services that you miss the opportunity to develop relationships.

People buy from people they like and from where they've had a good experience. They also tell their friends! Give customers an opportunity to provide customer feedback and mystery shop your team for a true customer experience.

Dust Collecting: Creating a 40-page business plan, putting it on a shelf and forgetting about it.

A true business plan should focus on maximizing your strengths, minimizing your weaknesses, seizing opportunities, and recognizing threats. It should have specific action items and should be reviewed continuously.

Marketing Misplacement: Treating marketing as a support function instead of a business strategy.

Ever hear of guerilla marketing? It's a war out there. Marketing is anything but passive. Just ask yourself what ever happened to Saab, General Cinemas, or McCall's magazine?

Penny Foolishness: Having no clear budget to market your product to your audience.

What good is a great product that no one knows about? Don't rely on luck to market your product or service. People say "you have to spend it to make it" because it's true. But you should also expect a return on every dollar you spend, so track results.

Following the Leader: Modeling your marketing plan after your competitors' instead of breaking away from the crowd.

Find your competitive advantage and focus all your efforts on it. Do everything you can to not be like everyone else.

Skeet Shooting: Reacting to whatever is presented without a clear method to gauge its relevance to your plan.

Your marketing plan will keep you on track to reach your goals through targeted, concentrated efforts. Use it!

Introspective Branding: Basing your brand's identity on what you think it is.

It's a hard pill to swallow but your brand is not determined by what you say it is. Your brand is what your customers think and say about your product and service. And, product quality isn't always the determining factor. It's often more about how people feel while using your product and how engaged they are with your brand.

SMIA – Social Missing in Action: Infrequent posting content on your social media pages.

If your last social media post was in 2009, you're giving the impression that you haven't had a desire to engage your audience, had anything of value to share, any new products or services to announce, any employees worth recognizing or customers worth celebrating in the last decade.

Inbound-phobia: Avoiding marketing channels you do not fully understand.

Marketing plans employing only traditional forms of marketing such as television, radio, and newspaper are expensive and ineffective. It's time to explore inbound marketing and reap the benefits of digital and social media marketing.

Media Envy: Placing expensive ads in publications dominated by "the big guys."

If your media budget isn't as big as theirs, you're wasting your money. Chances are you don't need to cast such a wide net anyway. Today's environment offers many highly targeted, less expensive ways to reach your audience.

Playing Doctor: Go ahead and perform your own surgery, replace your own fillings, diagnose your own illness. After all, you know your body better than any health care professional.

Don't try to market your company or product yourself. Let the experts help while you focus on running your business.

Marketing can be very tricky and full of hidden traps and opportunities to make a wrong turn. So, if you choose to venture into the marketing maelstrom without a trusted guide – good luck. You'll need it. But if you avoid these marketing pitfalls, you'll be off to a good start.

CHAPTER 6

Forget Back-to-School Sales. Get Back to Sales School.

To the legions of teens who slammed their books and lockers shut in June, the dreaded omens will soon begin appearing. Yes, in only a few weeks, back-to-school sales will be everywhere, warning screenagers who have spent the last 10 weeks binge-watching Riverdale, perfecting their gaming skills while saving Zelda and the kingdom of Hyrule, and attempting to mimic the fashion style of Kylie Jenner while working at Orange Julius – that it's time to return to the hallowed halls of learning.

But it's not just the kids who enjoy the lazy days of summer. With so many bosses, supervisors and clients on vacation, parents are also tempted to use their phones for social media updates rather than client calls, streaming Killing Eve rather than a webinar, and planning their World of Warcraft strategy before their revenue growth strategy.

Just as the kids must face dreaded back-to-school sales, we propose the adults get back to sales school. Knowing the answers to the following questions will prepare your business development team to be motivated and focused when their prospects return to their habitats of conference rooms and corner offices with next year's unspent budgets.

Have you reviewed the curriculum?

Do you have a strategic plan that outline the actions you need to take to be successful?

What courses will you need to take?

Does your sales team have the skills necessary to communicate benefits, overcome objections and close the sale?

What subjects are you good at?

What products or services do you offer that set you apart from the competition? If you don't have any then it is time to buckle down, hit the books and get one or two.

What's your major?

Who is going to be your target market and why? Do they have a need? Are they underserved? Are they in a position to purchase? Are they likely to be a long-term stream of revenue?

What supplies will you need?

Will you need an integrated campaign consisting

of public relations, social media, digital advertising, direct mail, print ads, and website landing pages, emails or a combination of a few select items?

Are you an A student or a C student?

What assessment or measurement systems do you have in place to track your progress?

By knowing the answers to these questions, you will be able to motivate your team to have a record-breaking sales season!

CHAPTER 7

Seven Tips to Improve Your Email Marketing

Email marketing is inexpensive and can be generated quickly and often. However, unless you approach it with the same thought and attention as an expensive multimedia campaign, you will get exactly what you pay for – very little. Be prepared to put in a little work if you want to get results.

1. Treat Your Database Like a Vending Machine.

If you want to get something good out of your database, you better be putting something good into it. Complete contact information for your clients, prospects, referral sources, and strategic partners that is coded so that emails can be targeted = a healthy, fruit-and-fiber bar. An excel sheet full of uncoded emails that was last updated in 2009 = a dusty bag of Funyuns stuck on the coil that refuses to drop.

2. Don't Incite. Be Insightful.

Your message should be appreciated, not abhorred. Don't be a salesperson. Be a resource. Use email marketing to provide clear tips that add value for your clients or prospects.

3. In the inbox, size matters.

Your message should be brief, but always include a link to your website for the voracious reader who just can't get enough of your industry wisdom.

4. Bonjour mes Amigos

Make sure you are sending the right message to the right people by properly coding your database. Your loyal longtime customers might be outraged to get an email offering deep discounts to new customers only.

5. What's Your Sign?

Just like a bad pick-up line, an ill-conceived subject line will turn off your reader. Your subject line should promise short, digestible information that is likely to be of interest.

6. No One Likes a Yahoo

People are less likely to open an email if they don't recognize the sender. Be sure to use an email address from your company's domain. An AOL or Yahoo address hints that your company is irrelevant.

7. Do You Have Post-Email Disorder?

Do you hit send and never look back? Check your email reports to see how many were opened. Conduct A/B Testing on subject lines and send times to determine effectiveness. Correct or delete bad addresses.

So don't underestimate the benefits of email marketing or lessen your efforts simply because it's inexpensive. Follow these seven rules and you'll soon experience a return on your investment few marketing platforms can offer.

CHAPTER 8

Unwritten Service Standards Aren't Worth the Paper They're Written On... Oh Wait.

Unwritten service standards. Those three words are as much of an oxymoron as jumbo shrimp. They are as useful as bringing sand to the beach, as effective as Congress, and make as much sense as being a little pregnant.

If a business cares enough about its customers to create service standards that ensure an exceptional customer experience every time, then they should be written, communicated and enforced.

For example, it's not enough that your team knows to answer the phone within three rings. They should also know which greeting you prefer they use. If not, your phone could be answered by an out-of-breath employee who dove for the phone only to answer with, *"Yo, Pete's Plumbing. Wassup? You leaking?"*

Requiring that your employees have an email signature is good. Telling them exactly what to include, line by line, is better. And, reminding them of what not to include such as political slogans, religious icons or even college or pro sport logos is awesome. No one cares that Gilbert in accounts receivable is a libertarian Scientologist and die-hard Norwegian curling team fan.

Requesting that your customers' emails and phone calls be returned in a timely matter is the equivalent to letting the inmates run the asylum. While most employees will understand that before the end of the day is a reasonable time frame, there's always some new-age free thinker in IT who wants to debate, *"What is time anyway, man? Let's not inflict ourselves with this self-imposed oppression."* Whatever — just return those emails. NOW!

Demanding that customers be greeted within seconds on entering your business is a good standard. However, unless you explain that an employee must also get up and walk over to the patron, you might as well give him license to shout, "Hey, I'm Jon. Let me know if you need anything," as the glow from his smartphone bathes his uncaring face and the click, click, click generated by his furiously texting digits fills the air. Let's face it, unless a customer wants to engage Jon in a friendly game of *Words with Friends*, his attention isn't available.

Eating in common areas. Chewing gum on the sales floor. Post-meeting correspondence. Proposal follow-up. These are just some of the many service standards that need to be clearly defined, communicated and enforced if they are going to make an impact on the customer experience you want your brand to deliver.

CHAPTER 9

Your Brand Is the Sum of Its Parts

Between my line of work and my circle of entrepreneurial-minded friends, I am often presented with ideas for new business ventures. I am almost always impressed at their innovative ideas and business acumen. However, I am equally surprised at how hung up they can get on one component of their brand, such as the logo or the name, when actually, a brand is the sum of its parts.

I am not saying that names and logos aren't important. You wouldn't name your accounting firm Embezzlers &

Associates nor should you select a baby seal cartoon as your logo. But, no one item should bear the responsibility of telling your brand's story. It's a team effort between the name, logo, font, color, tagline, marketing and collateral materials, website, online content and social media presence, just for starters.

Take Nike. By itself, what about that name means high performance athletic wear? Nothing.

Look at its logo or icon. What about that swoosh conveys hi-tech sports gear? Nothing.

Sure, its tagline, "JUST DO IT." brings to mind action – but let's face it – it could just as easily mean do your homework, quit your job, or make sweet whoopee.

Do you see where I am going with this? When you set out to establish your brand, you must decide the characteristics you want people to imagine when they think of your brand and then make every decision to support that goal.

Back to Nike. They use a sans serif font to be contemporary. Can you imagine if they used Old English? It wouldn't have the same impact would it?

Just Do It Thusly Ol' Chap!

Their website uses large bold action images of their products in use. It does not include stock images of a multi-ethnic group of office workers sitting around the conference table holding manila folders, pointing at a flip chart while pretending to use a calculator.

Their website employs words like limitless, dynamic, performance, revolutionary, effortless and epic. Although I didn't check, I am positive that the words lackluster, mediocre, humdrum, and average are nowhere on their website.

Nike's Facebook page includes an inspiring video of an octogenarian marathon runner. It does not feature any videos of animated sloths or migrating wildebeests.

Nike knows what it wants its brand to convey and makes each decision based on that. So should you. Just do it!

CHAPTER 10

All Employees Are Part of Your Marketing Team

It was 10 years ago, although it seems like only yesterday. The Electrum partners were meeting with a potential client and things were going well. The discussion was passionate. Ideas were plentiful. Strategies were forming. We were witnessing the genesis of a long-term partnership right before our very eyes! *Are those angels I hear singing?*

Then, without warning, the prospect reached into his drawer and pulled out his "logo," much like an assassin would draw his revolver. Let me say that we could not have been more surprised if he had produced a firearm, for this logo was equally frightening. Hand-drawn by his wife, the logo for his home décor product was comprised of the business name using a font made entirely of paint brushes. Yes, paint brushes! How innovative! How unique! How the heck are we going to make this work?

In the end, it didn't work. He was adamant that we use the logo as designed. We were adamant that logos should be legible.

We get it! Marketing can be a creative outlet to some people. A chance for accountants to stop crunching the numbers, for lawyers to put down their legal briefs, and for salespeople to postpone those sales calls. For entrepreneurs, marketing their business ideas can be very personal and extremely subjective – and therein lies the problem.

They are too close to the product to view it objectively. They are too familiar with its benefits to communicate them clearly. They describe their product using industry jargon and specs rather than elaborating on the benefits it offers. They assume that everyone will feel as they do and want their product before they've addressed what need it meets.

Like many professionals, marketers earn their degrees by studying core courses related to their industry such as principles of marketing, business-to-business marketing, consumer behavior, and market research. After years of real-world experience, many will go on to become experts in a specific area such as research analytics, search engine optimization, media planning, or public relations.

Unlike many professions, such as a lawyer who keeps you out of jail or a pilot who delivers you safely to your destination, marketing seems a less risky do-it-yourself project. But be warned, you may not end up serving 20 to life or crash into the ocean, but compromising a well-executed marketing plan with personal opinions and preferences could, over time, result in lost sales, decreased brand loyalty and a weakened brand image.

Again, we get it. People like to participate in

marketing and growing their business and we applaud them. Therefore, we've come up with three ways everyone can and should participate in marketing their business.

Focus on the Customer Experience (CX)

Be pleasant, knowledgeable, responsive, proactive, and respectful of your customer's time. Follow up accordingly. Be likeable. Make it impossible for them to want to do business with anyone else.

Be a Brand Ambassador

Practice your 30-second commercial so you can easily and effectively communicate what your business does and how you do it better than the competition, preferably with an example of how you've helped someone in their line of business. If you're not in sales, you can still generate leads for those who are.

Spread the Word

Establish your business as an industry expert and trusted resource by liking, sharing and commenting on its social media content related to your industry. It takes only seconds per day but can increase your brand's visibility exponentially. Have an idea for content? Share it with your marketing director. They will appreciate the input.

Want to expand your marketing team without increasing your payroll? Ensure that your employees are aware that they are expected to participate as outlined here – stressing that the company's success is directly connected to their paychecks and/or bonuses.

CHAPTER 11

Nectar for the News Feed Gods

In 2018, Facebook updated its news feed algorithm to deliver more content from friends and families and less from brands in order to ensure Facebook users have more meaningful social interactions.

While some brands reacted as if the sky is falling, Electrum applauded Mark Zuckerberg's effort to enhance the user experience. "I expect the time people spend on Facebook and some measures of engagement will go down," he said in his post about the changes. "But I also expect the time you do spend on Facebook will be more valuable."

So what can your brand do to ensure maximum opportunity to engage with your customers?

Create More Engaging Content

Post more videos or photos that showcase your brand's culture. But, keep it brief. Nobody wants a tour of your six-floor chia pet factory or view 89 photos of your call center team.

Answer questions your fans have. FYI: The answer

to, "Do these pants make my butt look big?" is ALWAYS no. *Trust me.*

Ask questions that start a dialogue. Do not ask about your pants.

Host and promote events that offer value. And, no, we do not mean Tupperware parties although a lettuce crisper is always an appreciated gift.

Get More Strategic

Evaluate which posts are performing well and replicate them. Meaning, post more photos of the customer service team dressed as Smurfs and fewer photos of the accounting team dressed as…well, accountants.

Know when your fans are most active on Facebook and post then, not at 3 a.m. when you can't sleep because you had a nightmare about the Facebook algorithm or costumed accountants.

Sponsor your content. According to Forbes, Facebook's ad revenue for Q3 2017 totaled $10.3 billion, so sponsored content is not going anywhere. Like any campaign, target your audience and message, set realistic goals, budget accordingly and measure results.

Encourage Your Employees to Be Advocates

It is estimated that the average brand post reaches only 2-5% of its followers, meaning that if 100 people "like" a brand page, only two to five of them are likely to see one of its posts. Your employees have the potential to be your single most valuable opportunity because they are trusted by their peers. By liking and sharing your brand's content, they are helping to increase the odds that it will be seen by their friends and family. And, since your employees are viewed as the source, the impressions they create generate better engagement.

Again, we applaud Facebook's efforts to deliver more meaningful social interactions. We just encourage you to follow our three rules to ensure those valuable engagements are with your brand.

CHAPTER 12

Use Common Sense When It Comes to Your Brand Messaging

In 1776, Thomas Paine's *Common Sense* was published. This pamphlet presented the American colonists with an argument for freedom from British rule and is credited with inspiring the population to declare their independence and fight.

Despite the trend at the time for writers to use philosophy and Latin references in their prose, Thomas Paine knew that in order to inspire the masses, he must follow a style and use language that common people understood.

Although he was not a religious man, he knew his audience was. Therefore, he relied on Biblical references to make his case to the people, writing Common Sense like a sermon. As a result, the pamphlet was a huge success, selling more than 500,000 copies in its first year. As a matter of fact, as of 2006, it was still credited as the all-time bestselling title of any book in American history (in relation to the size of the colonies at the time).

And, now, we arrive at the point of this chapter.

When it comes to your brand messaging, keep it simple.

- Be succinct. Keep your message simple and to the point. Why use 500 words when 100 or fewer will do?
- Use clear language that excites your audience. Avoid industry-specific lingo that only your colleagues understand.
- Avoid listing product specs. The technical capabilities may excite you, but what your audience wants to know is what they can expect as a result of using your product.
- Don't make the content all about you. Instead, your content should appeal to your audience's lifestyle and their aspirations. How can you make their life better? What role can you play in enhancing their lifestyle? Can you help them reach their goals?

What worked for our founding fathers to instill patriotism and start a revolution can work for your brand to instill passion and create loyalty.

CHAPTER 13

How to Create an Effective Tagline

"Sometime a scream is better than a thesis."
Ralph Waldo Emerson

At Electrum Branding, we couldn't agree more. A brief and powerful statement will always trump a lengthy and complex one. So, when it comes to your tagline — it should be brief, memorable and differentiate you from your competitors.

Your tagline should:

- Offer insight into your business, not be a summary of your business plan
- Refer to your product's key benefit, not a list of product specs
- Create a lasting impression of your brand, but only as part of a fully-executed marketing plan
- Never be written in stone. Just as your business changes, so should your tagline.

Although we cannot take credit for the iconic, "Just do it"; "When you care enough to send the very best" and "We try harder" — we pride ourselves on creating some very spot-on taglines for our clients, including:

A forensic accounting firm whose expertise has been instrumental in achieving many positive trial outcomes – **Strategies from numbers.**

A business that leads clients through the intimidating and esoteric industries of hedge funds and insurance – **Simplifying the complicated.**

An online eyeglass lens distributor who can quickly deliver discounted quality lenses – **Our vision is value.**

A financial institution that doesn't want to be considered just a bank, but rather a resource to get ahead – **Bank forward.**

A consulting firm that helps businesses improve their bottom line by eliminating the obstacles to going green – **Your blueprint for green.**

An independent community bank (with a nautical name) that offers many of the same products and services as the big banks – **Anchored in your community. Empowered to take you anywhere.**

And a branding agency that helps businesses find, get and keep customers through effective employee training, sales strategies, customer experience management, customer engagement, and online visibility – **Building your brand from the inside out.**

How well does your tagline measure up against these

winning tagline characteristics? Is it descriptive? Speak to a key benefit? Is it memorable?

CHAPTER 14

Five Tips for Delicious Customer Service

Tim Zagat's "Ten New Rules of Dining Etiquette," closes with, "The customer is always right. Expect hospitable, efficient service or take your money elsewhere…and then tell 10 people."

In today's rapid-fire, always connected world, telling hundreds of people about bad service is just as easy as telling 10. Regardless of whether your business is a restaurant, hotel, shoe store, or dry cleaner, ensuring that your employees are able to make your customers feel appreciated and well cared for should be a priority.

Be Prepared.

What's good for the scouts is good for your business too! Make sure that your staff isn't stretched so thin during peak hours that they are unable to provide exceptional customer service. If Evelyn calls in with another one of her "migraines," guess what? It's time for you to hit the sales floor and support your troops.

Benefits Sell. Specs Fail.

Make sure that your sales people are fully aware of all the product benefits and are comfortable communicating them to your customers. Anyone can read a list of product specs and features, and those same people should be placed in the backroom doing inventory.

A Little Knowledge Is a Dangerous Thing.

Make sure your staff is familiar with any and all specials. No one wants their lobster bisque to get cold while the waiter runs to the kitchen to see if the duck confit is fresh. By the way, the answer to that is always, "yes." *What else are you going to say?*

Create Problem Solvers

Empower your team to make decisions that can greatly impact the customer experience you offer. If the customer wants to switch hotel rooms because they want a better view, wants onion rings instead of fries, or wants to exchange an item for another size – your staff should be able to do so immediately with a smile rather than having to go ask their manager.

Feel Free to Help Yourself.

While most people like to be waited on, they are able to perform certain tasks perfectly fine on their own. Make the decision of how you can eliminate a few services in order to improve overall efficiency. If your shoe store is full of women waving peep-toe pumps, strappy sandals and kitten heels while yelling their shoe size, it's perfectly acceptable to deliver the shoes and move on to the next customer without going through the whole Cinderella-glass-slipper scenario.

The key ingredient in this recipe for exceptional customer service is training. Just like butter, you can never have enough.

CHAPTER 15

Don't Be Anti-Social

On any given day:

- More than a billion people use Facebook
- 500 million tweets are sent
- 95 million photos are shared on Instagram

By now, it's clear that social media is not a passing fad. What isn't clear is why more businesses are not embracing social media's ability to connect with their consumers, showcase their corporate culture, share helpful industry information, and so much more.

I confess that I know all too well why many businesses are hesitant, if not downright resistant, to taking their business social. I've heard all the excuses and, fortunately, I have all the answers.

We're afraid that unhappy customers will post negative comments.

Stop. Hold it right there. If unsatisfied customers are that plentiful, social media should NOT be a priority for your business, but customer experience training and measurement should be.

While the anticipation of negative feedback is often exaggerated, businesses should welcome customer comments – good and bad. There are several benefits to addressing customer service issues on social media:

1. It shows you are responsive and motivated to seek a solution.
2. The interaction gives you the opportunity to acknowledge the customer's frustration. This human touch is very effective at disarming a frustrated customer.
3. If you can keep the conversation online and can satisfy the customer, you're more likely to create a brand advocate.
4. If there is an issue such as a service outage, it provides you with a platform to proactively keep customers updated and informed of anticipated restoration.

What if our employees post inappropriate content on our business page?

If rogue employees are a concern, you might want to shift your focus to employee training before implementing a social media strategy. Actually, most businesses are relieved to learn that only designated administrators have the ability to create and post on a business's page. Despite this fact, employees should still be made aware of:

1. What is appropriate for them to include in post comments or shares
2. What they can do to leverage their business's social media efforts
3. How they can submit ideas for content

We don't have time to monitor Facebook all day.

Whew! If you did, we'd be worried. You can remain focused on running your business. Your admins are notified if anyone posts on your pages, shares, comments, or retweets. They can set aside a few minutes each day to address any issues if required. Or better yet, you hire a professional social media agency to manage this for you.

We could never come up with enough content.

Really? You can't think of something to say about your industry, your corporate culture, your employees, or your community support and create three to five posts each week? The fact is, most businesses find that, once they get started, they have an abundance of content to share.

Our audience isn't on social media.

Your industry may not be trending like The Bachelor but what is? With one in seven people on Earth using Facebook each day, your customers are using social media. Although finding and learning about your business may not be their intent, reaching them while they are connecting with their friends and seeking information should be yours.

We want to focus on Search Engine Optimization (SEO) before social media.

That's like saying you want to run the Boston Marathon wearing oversized galoshes. Twitter and Facebook boast a combined 2.6 billion search queries a day. Social and search go hand in hand in creating relevant, fresh content that people will find useful or entertaining – you can't have one without the other.

And finally, the comment that often goes unsaid, "We just don't understand it."

Hey, I don't know how to do a root canal, but I had one anyway. Just like you outsource web design, accounting and legal services, you can outsource your social media. Just because your seven-year-old niece can tweet, don't be ashamed for handing over your social media marketing strategy to the experts.

CHAPTER 16

A Customer Testimonial Has Many Benefits

If you are like the Electrum Branding team, you do your very best to ensure that your customers are satisfied. Actually, at Electrum, SATISFIED is the low end of the scale opposite MANIACALLY CONTENT – but that's a story for another day.

You must, of course, realize that you will not always succeed at achieving optimum customer satisfaction. But when you do, seize the opportunity and put your customer's euphoria to work for you. Carpe testimonium – or seize their testimonial *(loosely translated)* immediately! So why strive to secure testimonials?

They differentiate you from your competition.

If a prospect compares your print ad or website against your competitor's and all things are practically equal (*Have you seen the print ads for tires or mattresses?*), a heartfelt testimonial could tip the scales in your favor. Let's face it, if someone took the time to vouch for your service or product, it must be stellar, right?

They're good for your client's business as well.

When asking for a customer's testimonial, offer to include his or her business affiliation along with their testimonial on your promotional materials. If possible, illustrate how your exceptional product or service enabled them to improve their service delivery. Now, you're both winners! OMG – *this just keeps getting better right?*

You may learn something.

You may think you know why your customer uses your services, but often the answers to a few open-ended questions such as *"Why do you continue to use our services?"* and *"What do you like best about our services?"* might be eye-opening for you. You may think they appreciate the extra cheese you put on their sandwich only to learn it's your quick service and convenient location. UGH! Think of all that cheese you've wasted! By promoting the benefits that happy customers enjoy, you can attract more happy customers and drive revenue.

You may establish a referral source.

Strike while the iron's hot. Ask your satisfied customer to refer business to you. And, if they're happy, they probably know someone else that you could also please.

If they say no, then move on. Know that they're lying, but move on. If they say yes, then hand them a stack of your business cards or fliers and send them on their way.

In the time you read this, you've likely identified a few satisfied clients you would like to approach. So, don't delay. Carpe testimonium!

CHAPTER 17

Search Engines Are Not Evil

For those of us whose professional focus is to rank well in online search results, search engine giants such as Google and Bing may, at times, seem to be omnipotent oligarchs hell bent on keeping us confounded with hundreds upon hundreds of algorithm updates each year.

But nothing could be further from the truth. Just like any business owner, their goal is to provide users with a satisfying experience to nurture brand loyalty. They know that if the search results they provide leave the user unsatisfied, that user will search elsewhere.

To help you better understand how search works, here's an overly simplified explanation of several factors and how they influence search results.

Search engines employ software called "spiders" to continuously crawl the internet, indexing and re-indexing web pages…billions of pages. So, when someone searches for Hugh Jackman, the search engines pull any page that references "Hugh" or "Jackman."

Knowing that you don't want to sort through pages

devoted to Hugh Hefner, Hugh Laurie, Jackman Fabrics or Jackman, Maine, the search engines rank pages, placing the ones most relevant to your search closest to the top. Below are only a few examples of the hundreds of factors that affect search results.

Keyword Proximity

If a page mentions "Hugh Jackman" rather than "Hugh Laurie recommends Jackman Fabrics," the first site is placed higher than the latter.

Keyword Density

A page that mentions Hugh Jackman in the headline and then several times in the copy, will rank higher than a site that only mentions his name in the cast credits.

Freshness of Content

If a website's latest Hugh Jackman entry reviews his 1999 depiction of Curly in the made-for-TV production of *Oklahoma*, it won't rank as high as a website covering his latest performance in *Logan*.

Links to Website

A website with information on Hugh Jackman that receives links from *Entertainment Weekly* or TMZ, will rank infinitely higher than one with a sole link from the Worldwide Wolverine Whitepaper, a blog written by a middle-aged former D&D dungeon master living in his parent's basement.

Age of Website

The older your site, the more reliable the search engines will perceive it to be.

Site Traffic

The more web traffic you have, the more popular your website will be perceived.

Social Media Engagement

If a website's content is being liked, shared and retweeted, search engines will consider your content to be fresh, relevant and engaging.

So, the next time you conduct a search query, take a moment to marvel at the quality of information that is returned to you in less than a second. Mind blowing isn't it? FYI – More than 305 million results for "mind blowing" were just returned in six-tenths of a second.

CHAPTER 18

Does Your Website Need a Cosmetic Update or a Complete Overhaul?

In today's digital age, your website is often the face of your business. It can make the first impression, develop leads and generate sales. Given its vital role in your success, it is critical that it effectively communicate and fortify your brand.

So how can you tell if your website is performing at its peak? Could it benefit from a slight cosmetic update or does it need a more strategic overhaul? Below are a few questions to help you decide.

Is your website a road map or a maze?

Is your website easy to navigate? Nothing on your website should be more than three clicks from the home page. That requires a well-planned site map with content that is organized in a manner that makes sense to the viewer. If people can't find what they are looking for on your site, they'll look elsewhere.

Is your website lost or found?

Is your site optimized for search engines? With more than 5.6 billion searches queried on Google every day, more than likely a prospect is searching for your product or services. If you're not showing up in the search results, you can bet your competition is.

Is your website looking fine at any size?

Is your website employing responsive web design (RWD)? The surge in tablet and smart phone popularity has resulted in a dramatic drop in the use of PCs. RWD ensures that your website looks its best whether it's viewed on a desktop, smart phone or tablet.

Is your website dynamic or dated?

Does your website have a contemporary design? Since viewers are looking for current, relevant content, they'll choose a contemporary looking website over a dated site any day. Modern websites are designed with higher resolutions to fit larger PC monitors, larger bolder images and more engaging content that viewers want to read and share.

Is your website mobile or stuck?

Does your website require users to complete forms or make purchases? If so, a dedicated mobile site is recommended since 76% of surveyed consumers said they wouldn't bother using a site not optimized for mobile and 30% would turn to a competitor's site that was. Mobile optimized sites are designed for faster download speed, easier navigation, and require less expanding and shrinking of content resulting in a greater user experience.

Is your website anti-social?

Are you savvy enough to be taking advantage of the branding power of social media? If so, your website should feature social media icons with links to your pages to increase customer engagement.

How well did your website stand up to these six questions? As a highly visible member of your sales team, you should expect nothing less from your website than you do your top salespeople. When they need resources, training, or sales collateral, you provide it. Don't deny your website the tools it needs to be a successful lead generator.

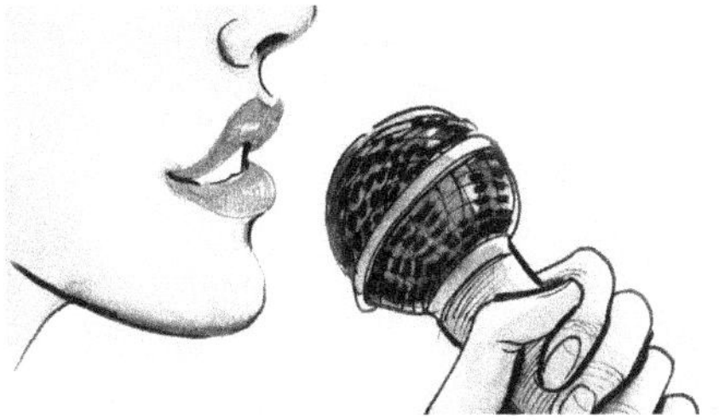

CHAPTER 19

Word of Mouth Marketing: Putting Words in Your Customer's Mouth

Long gone are the golden days of advertising, when consumers accepted advertising as gospel. Doctors promoting the health benefits of Camel cigarettes? *Of course!* Moms elated to find Hoover vacuums under their Christmas trees? *Obviously!* And, pure and wholesome 7-Up for infants? *No doubt about it!*

However, that naive gullibility has gone the way of landline phones, network-only television, and cursive writing. In a 2017 Gallup poll, 34% of US adults surveyed rated the honesty and ethical standards of advertising practitioners as low or very low, placing marketers just above members of Congress, car salespeople, and lobbyists. Now, please excuse me while I go shower. I feel dirty.

In contrast, according to Nielsen, 92% of people trust recommendations from friends and family over any other type of advertising. In response, strategic brands are embracing word-of-mouth marketing – personal referrals amplified through social media.

By implementing a few strategies, brands can not only get their audience talking, but can influence what is being said as well. And, with 74% of consumers identifying word of mouth as a key influencer in their purchasing decisions, it's a conversation worth influencing.

Online Reviews

According to BrightLocal, 85% of people trust online reviews as much as they trust personal contacts and positive reviews make 73% of customers trust a business more. Here are a few tips for securing business reviews.

- Create an online profile on sites where people are likely to search for product or service information such as Yelp, Facebook, Google (Google My Business), Amazon, Better Business Bureau and others.
- Make it easy for people to post reviews by creating links to sites mentioned above by placing links on your website, social media and email marketing.
- Invite people to write a review at the end of their positive customer experience, after they've posted something positive on social media, or if they refer business your way.

Promote a Unique Hashtag

Create a specific hashtag (#) for your brand, product or special event and promote the selected hashtag on social media, in-store signage, catalogs, selfie stations and more.

By providing an official hashtag, you're inviting people to post and ensuring that they do it uniformly for greater impact. To promote Fort Lauderdale tourism, photo opportunities around town were branded with #PlayLauderdale – resulting in more than 1,000 images on Instagram alone of people having fun in Fort Lauderdale.

Create Contests

Ask followers to submit reviews for a chance to be featured in a customer profile on your website or newsletter. Alert followers to the fact that photos tagged with a specific hashtag will be considered for use in your next print ad. Ask followers to submit photos for cutest puppy, messiest desk, most glamorous holiday decor – something related to your brand. The opportunities are endless. Just be sure contests are designed to achieve a goal such as collecting email addresses, website visits, newsletter subscriptions, or adding social media followers.

Encourage Reviews and User Generated Content (UGC)

Customers are likely to continue promoting your brand and encouraging others to do the same if they feel it is valued. Let them know it is by sharing their positive reviews on your website or social media. Repost their Instagram images and share their Facebook photos. Create an incentive program offering a gift card or discount if a certain number of their photos are selected and reposted or shared to your page.

Provide a Product or Service that's Shareworthy

Last, but certainly not least, create an experience that your customers can't help but rave about. If you don't, your reviews are likely to be lackluster and user photos few and far between. Make the experience your priority and positive word of mouth will occur organically. However, combine that experience with a clear plan to share it with others, and the sky's the limit.

CHAPTER 20

Presentation Is Everything

Business development is highly competitive. As such, it's imperative that you are selling your brand at every opportunity – email, website, social media, direct mail, print and digital advertising…and, of course, your proposals.

If you're a plumber, you may not think the look of your proposal matters as long as the content is accurate, and your price is fair. Wrong. How your proposal looks and how the information is presented can influence the decision makers just as easily as the price.

To ensure that you are maximizing every opportunity to sell your brand, Electrum Branding has prepared the following proposal tips.

Follow Instructions

If you are responding to a request for proposal (RFP), be sure you provide the proposal before the deadline, with copies provided exactly as requested, and with the information presented in the order it was requested. If you can't follow these instructions, how can you be expected to retrofit the plumbing in a 19th century monastery?

Keep Up Appearances

Presenting a carefully formatted proposal shows that you took the decision-maker's monumental task of reviewing scores of proposals into consideration. By adding photos when appropriate and formatting the text with bulleted lists and bold headings, you can make consuming information much easier while ensuring the most important information isn't missed.

Own the Goal

Make their goal the centerpiece of your proposal by including how you will help achieve it in every section of your proposal. Prove that you want to be their partner, not just a vendor.

Do Your Homework

Do a deep dive into the prospect's recent history as well as the current environment of their industry. Including this summary in your proposal shows you have an idea of their strengths, weaknesses, opportunities, and threats.

Don't Take Our Word for It

"Visit our website for a few customer testimonials"... said no one EVER! Place a few testimonials that reference the services you are selling throughout your proposal. If you are pitching your accounting services and you have a client who raves about the accuracy and thoroughness of your bookkeeping, it should be prominently featured.

Recent Industry Distinctions

If you have been recognized as a leader in your industry, it probably wasn't due to your modesty so why start now? Be sure to mention all recent industry awards, distinctions or milestones in your proposal. Recent is the key word here. Industry, too. No one wants to see your perfect attendance certificate from vacation Bible school circa 1975.

Reporting

Provide samples of how you will report on your progress along with a reporting schedule. This will illustrate what kind of data you provide and how important results are to you.

Process

Including your work process and service standards shows that you have a work process and service standards. Also, if you share a few of the same service standards — ding, ding, ding — points for you!

Personality and Culture

Your proposal may be for the prospective client, but it represents your business.Therefore, it should look like you and sound like you. Showcase your corporate culture and feature the people on your team with whom they will be working.

It's Not All about You

Your pride in your business may cause you to overshare, but don't. Keep the focus on the skills and services you possess to help them reach their goals. There'll be plenty of time to learn more about your business after the contract is signed.

Pricing

After the negotiations begin, you can only go down in price, so start at the high end of your range. However, be careful here. No one wants to hear, "Let me see if I can get back to you with a better price."

An Objective Eye

Is your proposal jargon free? Is it easy to understand? Do yourself a favor and have a trusted peer outside your industry review your proposal to ensure your content is clear and positions your brand favorably.

By following these 12 proposal tips, you can ensure your proposal stands out from the rest while effectively illustrating your desire and ability to play a role in your prospect's success.

CHAPTER 21

What's Haunting Your Brand?

Halloween is one of my favorite holidays. In addition to the costumes and the bowlfuls of candy, Halloween is the official start of the holiday season. Yes, in the months following All Hallows Eve, we run the gamut of emotions from Halloween fright and Thanksgiving gratitude to Christmas joy and New Year optimism.

Although I experience a myriad of emotions every day, these feelings are amplified during holiday season since they come complete with costumes, decorations, music, parties, cocktails, and culinary feasts.

With Halloween on my mind, I've prepared a list of scary brand failures that may be haunting your brand.

Zombies

Businesses that operate without marketing plans which provide measurable goals, defined tactics and set strategies are like zombies. They wander aimlessly, changing direction only when they hit an obstacle or get distracted by a shiny object.

The Invisible Man

A business whose website has not been optimized for search might as well be invisible since no one will ever see it. And, although visible, a website without responsive web design can be maddening when viewed on a mobile device.

Haunted House

If social media pages could collect dust, some businesses' social media pages would resemble Miss Havisham's parlor (Google it). An unattended social media page is as inviting as a decaying haunted house.

Frankenstein's Monster

To save money, some businesses piece together marketing materials composed of bits and pieces of previous marketing pieces. The results are often worthy of the pitchfork and torch-wielding reception they receive.

Jack-o-Lanterns

Clients can be all smiles at your presentation, only to turn rotten, squishy and a little smelly when it comes time to execute your cutting-edge idea. Fear of looking different than the competition can be terrifying to some businesses.

The Grim Reaper

Unlike the Jack-o-Lantern, the Grim Reaper is

negative from the get-go. At least you know what you are dealing with from the beginning, a nay-sayer who is averse to change with, "That's the way we've always done it" cross stitched on his sofa pillows.

Don't scare off business by allowing any of these brand failures to haunt your brand. *Exorcise* your right to an effective brand strategy and you'll be up to your hat buckle in new business by Thanksgiving.

CHAPTER 22

Four Things Santa Can't Live Without

The holidays are a magical time. In the span of nine weeks, we are given the opportunity to do things we can only do during the holidays including:

- Blaming our rabid consumption of miniature candies on trick-or-treaters that never came
- Debating on whether it's called stuffing or dressing as well as the merits of fresh cranberry sauce versus the congealed wiggly stuff in the can
- Secretly listening to "All I Want for Christmas Is You" on repeat while eating a tin of sugar cookies
- And making plans for an Instagrammable New Year's Eve so we can feel better about spending the rest of the year on the sofa

But while we're enjoying the spirit of the season, Santa is hyper-focused on the myriad of tasks that lie ahead. Thank goodness he knows he can rely on a few trusty tools to ensure a stellar performance on his big night.

Customer Testimonials

Nine out of 10 mall Santas agree: A mom telling Santa that her child has been a good little boy or girl carries a lot more weight than that child's own evaluation of his or her questionable behavior. Your customers feel the same. Endorsements from their peers are a lot more effective than flowery brochure copy or generic "we give great service" claims.

Marketing Plans

In order for Santa to deliver toys to all the good boys and girls in one night, he must create, implement and adhere to a detailed logistics plan. Any deviation and he might skip Papua New Guinea altogether or run out of toys before he gets to Tonga.

As a business owner with fewer resources and a lot less pixie dust than Santa, you must focus your limited resources on projects that will deliver the biggest results. Following a marketing plan enables you to prioritize and prevent distractions such as special media pricing or unsolicited input from a new board or team member from diverting your focus. As you measure results along the way, you can always fix what isn't working.

Customer Experience (CX) Management and Measurement

How many times have you seen Santa listening to

a child's wish list and thought "great customer feedback?" *Just me? Really?* By listening to his customers, Santa is simply giving the people what they want – and keeping them coming back for more. And, no brand audit is necessary since his brand is solid: identifiable wardrobe, signature laugh, one-of-a-kind transportation, and a gig that gets raves year after year from throngs of adoring fans.

However, unlike Santa, you have competition and your customers aren't nearly as loyal. A customer experience (CX) measurement and management program including a brand audit, customer surveys and mystery shopping can help improve service delivery, heighten customer loyalty and drive repeat sales.

Outsourcing

Imagine if Santa had to make all the toys himself. It's exhausting just thinking about it. Fortunately, he understands the benefits of outsourcing his toy making to the elves.

More and more companies are realizing the benefits of outsourcing services such as payroll and bookkeeping. And, for most small businesses, it makes sense to outsource their marketing as well. The benefits of outsourcing your marketing to a full-service agency include expert talent, significant cost-savings, and brand consistency. Plus, you also enjoy the convenience of a one-stop shop versus multiple vendors.

Ready to take your business from the naughty to nice list? Then be like Santa and employ these tried and true methods to ensure a brand performance that's worth celebrating all year long.

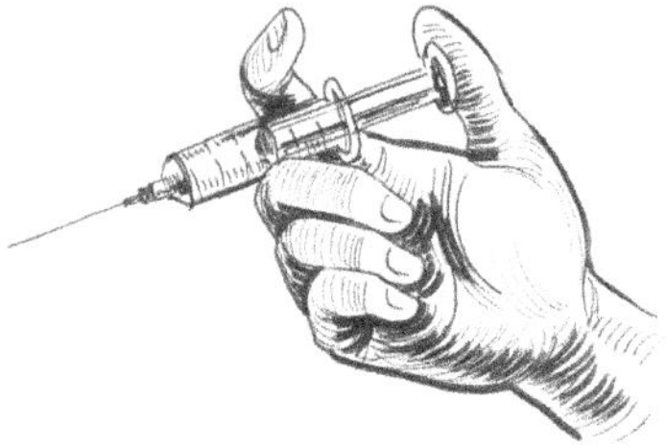

CHAPTER 23
The Brand Doctor Is In

Do you suffer from selfie elbow, text claw or iPad hand? Although these may not be official medical diagnoses yet, the writing's on the wall. There are reports and studies describing the consequences our obsession with our tech devices and the havoc repetitive motions and overuse can cause to our hands, fingers and elbows.

This motivated the brand doctors at Electrum Branding to release our own report on recent brand-related conditions that seem to be appearing with greater frequency and their possible treatments.

Brand Blindness

Caused by thinking that your brand consists of your logo, your newspaper ad or your website while it is actually none of those things. Your brand is the impression left in the minds of your prospects and customers at every touchpoint, including how your employees answer the phone and the cleanliness of your bathrooms as well as the quality of your product and the efficiency of your service.

The cure: Implementing a mystery shopping program can provide objective insight that will enable you to improve on the specific behaviors that increase customer satisfaction, sales and profitability while eliminating actions that are deterring repeat business.

Marketing Instinct

The belief that because you know what commercials you like and can identify a print ad when you see one, you can develop and execute a fully realized brand strategy.

The cure: Hire a professional. You wouldn't cut your own hair or perform your own surgery, so why entrust how you communicate your services to your target audience to your receptionist or human resources department? The money invested in a professional should more than pay for itself. If not, you hired the wrong professional.

The Response You Want Versus The Response You Need

Being complacent with a handful of positive customer feedback cards and assuming the other 99% of your customers feel the same. Don't wait to find out about customer dissatisfaction by reading negative online reviews.

The cure: Customer feedback surveys can discover opportunities to turn merely satisfied customers into raving fans.

Focus Group of One

Using your own opinion as a case study. For example, you don't use Snapchat, therefore, no one uses Snapchat. Just an FYI: As of June 2019, the app had 203 million daily users, with 3+ billion snaps sent every day.

The cure: Research. Find out where your audience is gathering information that influences their buying behaviors and build a presence in that space.

So what's ailing your brand? Just like any illness, the sooner you treat the symptoms the better. Don't wait until the prognosis is terminal, take action now.

CHAPTER 24

Blog Away Business Blandness

It's perfectly fine for your business not to have a blog. Many people feel this way. Of course, they are likely the same people who never raised their hand in class, wore a beige gown with ecru accents to prom, and never took on optional homework for extra credit. It's possible that this need to blend in to the point of being invisible served these people well, but who knows. They disappeared after graduation and have not been heard from since.

My point is this: What's good for the classroom chameleon is not good for your business. In today's highly competitive digital world, a blog can be a very effective tool for a variety of reasons.

- A blog can establish your business as a trusted resource in your industry.
- A blog can give your business personality.
- A blog can help you compete with businesses with marketing budgets exponentially larger than yours.
- A blog can add your voice to trending, timely online conversations.

- A blog can be a continuous source of fresh keyword-rich content for your website.

Raise Your Hand.

By writing about your industry and providing useful information on trending topics in a timely manner, you can, over time, establish yourself as a valued resource that people trust. By focusing on being insightful and helpful rather than selling, you can build a reputation as a reliable authority. And, because it's your blog, you control the content, the timing of its release, and its tone. Even a tummy-sculpting Spanx doesn't offer you this much control, so seize the opportunity.

Ditch the Beige.

Your blog can give your business personality. Although you may have a traditional product in a conservative industry, there's nothing preventing you from injecting a little humor into your blog as long as the content is accurate and useful. Believe me, people will remember where they read a humorous take on asset management or supplemental health benefits. Keep in mind that you don't always have to write about your services. You can brag about a successful client outcome you achieved, introduce your team, or rave about a client. Just be interesting!

Go for Extra Credit.

With more than 63,000 Google searches every

second, there's no denying that the internet has become our primary source for information. Therefore, ranking well in search results is crucial. When done properly, search engine optimization (SEO) can level the playing field between a small business with a modest marketing budget and a regional chain with a marketing budget that makes Madison Avenue salivate. Although search engines change the algorithms that affect their rankings almost daily (and mostly in secret), keywords, incoming links, indexed pages, fresh content, and social media "likes" and "shares" continue to impact search results. A blog provides you with all of the above.

So seize the opportunity and begin blogging away business blandness. Just be prepared to stand out from the competition while establishing your business as a trusted resource with greater online visibility. And, if your high school reunion is coming up, start shopping for something in chartreuse, magenta, or multi-colored sequins – anything but beige.

CHAPTER 25
Will Your Elevator Speech Raise You Up or Take You Down?

An elevator speech, elevator pitch, or 30-second commercial – whatever you want to call it, can often be your opportunity to make a remarkable first impression. But just as often, it can uh…be a rambling uh… bit of uh… nonsensical uh…confusing uh…networking sadism inflicted upon captive audiences by a handful of Marquis de Sades who didn't prepare prior to the chamber breakfast. *You know who you are.*

In addition to being an effective way to make it clear to a prospect what you do, how you do it better than the competition, and how your clients benefit – a proper 30-second commercial conveys respect for other people's time. If you pique their attention, they will ask for more detail. Give everyone the opportunity to first find out what everyone does so we can network judiciously after the event.

Do not, I repeat, do not attempt to establish yourself as an accounting expert by reciting your knowledge of the new tax codes – international and domestic – before someone wrestles the microphone from your cold, abacus-blistered fingers.

Chamber luncheons, corporate cocktail parties, and even actual elevators can present you with the opportunity to deliver your elevator speech so be prepared. Practice. Practice. Practice…and then deliver it like you're saying it for the first time.

1. Say what you do and who you do it for
2. State how you do it better than your competition
3. Give an example of how your clients benefit from working with you
4. And, close with an offer or invitation

For example: Electrum Branding is a branding agency that helps businesses find, get and keep customers. Although we design clever ads and cutting-edge websites, we're more than an advertising agency – we're branding experts focused on cost-effective branding strategies that get results for our clients. We always answer our phones and return emails so contact me if you would like more customers today.

What would happen if you suddenly found yourself face to face with your top prospect who politely asked, "What do you do?" Would you rattle off a laundry list of services rather than benefits? Would you present too much irrelevant detail? Would you talk in circles? Would you forget to ask for his or her business?

Don't be caught unprepared. Practice your responses to the four items above and be ready when the opportunity arises to deliver your elevator speech that will take you straight to the penthouse.

CHAPTER 26

A Logo Gets the Last Laugh

A few years have passed since the monumental tragedy. People have moved on. The healing has begun. No, we're not talking about climate change, deadly hurricanes, destructive wildfires, mass shootings or the Trump presidency. No, we are talking about the new Instagram logo. (Gasp) – *Is it too soon?*

On May 11, 2016, Instagram changed its logo from an icon resembling a Polaroid camera of the 1970s to something reminiscent of The Electric Kool-Aid Acid Test of the 1960s – and, the world went understandably mad. Immediately, blogs by the thousands – I mean hundreds of thousands – began to hit the internet heralding the new logo as a "travesty," "sad and disappointing," and "design gone awry." *The New York Times* called it, "The Great Instagram Logo Freakout of 2016."

In addition to the blogs condemning the change in design, online articles began to appear with complex instructions for beating the system in order to display the old icon on your smartphone or tablet. Really? Do Instagram users have jobs? Families? Are they not binge-watching Black Mirror? I mean, who has this much time on their hands?

The fact is, some people get very excited about design and may feel slighted if a design they were fond of gets a makeover when they thought it was perfectly fine. *What do others see that I don't?*

Others put too much emphasis on the logo and expect its design to carry the responsibility of communicating the brand. A perfect example is when Enterprise Florida, an organization whose focus is promoting Florida's job growth, unveiled its logo featuring a necktie in place of the letter 'I' in 'Florida.' What was meant to convey a business focus was labeled offensive, sexist and sinister by many critics. Not since the yellow silk power tie of the 1980s has a single tie garnered so much attention.

FLORIDA

The Perfect Climate For Business.

The fact is, your brand is the sum of many parts so the design alone simply doesn't matter. (Cue needle off the record scratch here.) Yes, fat letters, thin letters, italics, squares, circles…they won't make or break your business.

- A logo doesn't increase your visibility. Your marketing does.
- A logo doesn't increase sales. Your people and your messaging do.
- A logo doesn't build loyalty. Your product quality and customer service do.
- A logo doesn't build a strong corporate culture. That's management's task.

Granted a logo isn't worthless when it comes to your brand image. In fact, it is the visual representation of your brand. Therefore, it should be memorable and relevant to your corporate name, image or service. For instance, if you're a technology company, a butter churn may not be best image for your logo.

- A logo should enhance your corporate image. Translated, this means DO NOT USE COMIC SANS. Ever!
- A logo should work in all media. What looks great on a billboard may be unintelligible on a business card.
- A logo should not be a cliché. Law firms should avoid using scales. Medical practices, caducei.
- And for Pete's sake, can we please ban swooshes for all industries already?

It's doubtful that Instagram lost many users over the logo update and likely gained several thousand new customers as a result of the publicity. In fact, following all the hysterical publicity surrounding the Instagram logo, the number of Instagram users has grown from 500 million in 2016 to one billion today. And why? Because the social and marketing benefits of the app were never suspect – only the subjective appeal of the design was called into question at the time.

See, a logo isn't everything.

CHAPTER 27

Five Tips to Maximize Your Online Ad Campaign

If you have not already tried the highly targeted and cost-effective world of pay-per-click (PPC) advertising, it's time to dip your toe in the digital pool. Benefits of PPC advertising include a small investment to get started, complete control over your monthly budget, ability to track results and target specific geographic areas — and you only pay when someone is interested and clicks on your ad. Compare that with a newspaper ad for which you pay full price regardless if anyone wants your book, "Crafting with Cat Hair." *Yes, that is a thing!*

But, before you leap off the 15-meter diving platform and cannonball into the world of internet marketing, follow these five tips to maximize your PPC's ROI.

1. Run a Negative Campaign

Negative keywords are the most underused features offered for PPC campaigns. Negative keywords are words that are often associated with your topic but are completely irrelevant to your product. By employing negative keywords, you can prevent your ad from appearing and receiving worthless clicks. For example, when marketing "Crafting with Cat Hair," add "allergies," "removal" and "shedding" to your negative keyword list to reduce your clicks and save your PPC dollars.

2. Location, Location, Location

Google and Bing offer geo-location features, which allow you to target geographic markets based on IP addresses, geo-specific keywords or both, giving you the ability to target Calico, CA; Tabby Island, GA; Kitty Hawk, NC; or any place in between.

3. Curiosity Won't Kill This Cat

Pique your prospects' interest by offering value and then capitalizing on it with a clear call to action. Use terms like "Learn More" and "Free Download" to draw in customers. For instance, when marketing "Crafting with Cat Hair," you might want to offer "Free Psychiatric Evaluations."

4. Utilize Long-Tail Keywords

Long-tail keywords are three-to-four-word phrases that are specific to your product. Visitors using very specific search phrases are often further along in the purchasing process and can result in a higher conversion rate. For example, use "Crafting with Cat Hair" instead of just "crafting," "cat," or "hair."

5. A Homepage Is Not a Landing Page

When tossed in the air, it is said that a cat will always land on its feet. However, a prospect who clicks on your ad should not land on your website's home page. Like a cat chasing a laser beam, consumers confuse easily and are easily distracted. Deliver them to a landing page that picks up right where your PPC ad left off. Don't lose your visitor — and potential sale — by confusing them with unnecessary content.

Ready to get started or still hesitant? Don't be a scaredy cat. As stated earlier, PPC campaigns are easy to manage, easy to pause, and easy to update. There are as many ways to finesse your PPC campaign as there are ways to skin a cat.

CHAPTER 28

Eight Remedies for Sickly Email Results

Have your email marketing results been sickly? Any idea why? Although you may be tempted to blame the overwhelming number of emails that flood inboxes daily and the ease in which they can be deleted, don't.

A report by HubSpot cites that email marketing remains the most effective digital marketing channel for customer retention in the US. The report also claims that 59% of business-to-business (B2B) marketers say email is the most effective channel for generating revenue and 49% of B2B marketers spend more time and resources on email than on other channels.

So then, what's ailing your email efforts? Follow this diagnostic checklist and get your email on the road to recovery.

1. It's Not All About You

When it comes to subject lines, "Our January Banking Newsletter" is as effective as, "Our Annual Family Holiday Newsletter" for getting email opened and read.

Don't be offended, but no one cares about you. They care about what you can do for them. Give them a reason to open your email by offering tips or asking questions that intrigue them. However, be careful to avoid spammy words such as buy, free, save, sale, discount, % off, guarantee, discount, and above all – never use the word Viagra…at least not in your subject line.

2. Greetings from the Unknown

Will your recipients recognize the name of your email's sender? Use your full brand name (do not abbreviate) and never use No-Reply@YourDomain.com. The latter sends a clear message that you're only interested in one-way communication.

3. More is Less Effective

No one wants to read several, or even one, long rambling article. Present the viewer with an intriguing teaser and a link to read more. If they want to read more (and, of course, they will), they will click through to the full article which should reside on your website.

4. Make an Appearance

If your email is all text with little or no design at all, you run the risk of no one reading it. Using a clunky template will make you look unprofessional. Even using a professional design that looks nothing like your brand will likely confuse your reader. Email software has come a long way and now creating a template that reflects your brand is easy. Easier still is to have a marketing professional create a template for you.

5. Hold the Phone

According to a Fluent survey, 75% of respondents said they use their smart phone most often to check emails. Therefore, make sure your email is not only legible on a smart phone, but ensure that links are easily found and your call to action is impossible to miss.

6. Testing One, Two, Three

If your message is worth sending, then it's worth sending right. View your email on Chrome, Safari, Firefox and Edge. What works well on one browser can look askew on another. Do the same with smart phones and tablets. Then, when you are ready to send, test your subject line by dividing your list and sending to segments using different subject lines and see if there is a noticeable difference in the open rates.

7. The Personal Touch

Your message should be relevant to your audience. Although sending an email promoting pool supplies in January makes perfect sense to your customers in Florida, it will make you look disconnected to your Michigan customers.

Segment your lists and create content accordingly.

8. Read 'em and Weep

Of course, in the end, if your content isn't informative, compelling or entertaining — your email and your brand reputation may be DOA.

CHAPTER 29

Video Allows Your Brand to Be Seen and Heard

What do you think of when you hear the word video? Are you reminded of the birth of MTV and its proclamation that video killed the radio star? Or do you recall heading to Blockbuster on a Friday night hoping that one of its 47 copies of "Die Hard" would still be available? Or perhaps you regret the hour you wasted watching "Gangnam Style" repeatedly on YouTube?

Regardless of how you used to think of video, if you have a business to market, you need to rethink your perception of video. In the past five years, the pervasiveness of video and its importance in boosting a website's search engine rankings, online conversions, email marketing results, and brand credibility has risen dramatically.

According to sources:

- Including video on landing pages can increase conversion rates by over 80%. (Hubspot)
- The mere mention of the word "video" in your email

subject line increases open rates by 19%. (Hubspot)

- 90% of customers say that videos help them make buying decisions. (Hubspot)
- Video drives a 157% increase in organic traffic from search engine result pages (SERP). (Wordstream)
- Video will represent 82% of all internet traffic in 2021. (Business Insider)

Although you may not be in a visual industry such as fashion, interior design or entertainment, there is no doubt you have something to communicate that's done better through video rather than text and still photography. Even if you produce and market rolls of adding machine paper – there's a video for you.

Demo Videos

Show how your product works. Show how to assemble it. Compare your product against the competition. Show shortcuts and useful hints that may be hard to follow in an instruction manual.

Brand Videos

Build awareness of your brand beyond the services you offer by telling your brand story. What is your mission? What are your values? Why does your company exist? What excites you?

Event Videos

If you want to establish your business as a resource, videos of your business facilitating a roundtable or hosting a conference are ideal.

Expert Interviews

By conducting and taping interviews with experts from your business or from a strategic partner, you will add value for the viewer while building trust within your industry.

Explainer Videos

Some products and services are simply too complex to read about. However, by walking the viewer through the product or services with concise, easy-to-follow copy and creative video, the viewer can easily comprehend what you are offering.

Case Study and Customer Testimonial Videos

One of the best ways to prove your worth is by featuring satisfied, loyal customers who can effectively share the issue they experienced and the solution you provided. It sounds much more believable when someone else says how great you are.

So now that you are sold on the value of video, here are a few things to consider.

Video production need not be expensive.

Gone are the days where video production required a director, art director, hair and make-up artist, boom operator, and sound mixer. *Exactly what is a best boy, gaffer and a key grip anyway?* Today's videos can be shot from a smartphone. In the end, it's not how the video was shot but the quality of the final edited product that's important.

Simple can be engaging.

Videos do not have to have lots of effects to be entertaining. In fact, too many bells and whistles can take away from your message. Unless of course you're selling bells and whistles, then in that case, never mind.

It may be your video, but it's not about you.

The focus of your video should be your viewer. How can they relate to your product or service? How do you address a problem or issue they have? How are you better than the competition? How do you make them look good or their life easier?

Size does not matter.

If you can make your case in 15 seconds and leave the viewer impressed, good for you! However, most brands will take longer and that's fine, too. Just be aware of your viewer's attention span, possible time limitations, and other screens vying for their attention. Whatever the length, make every second entertaining, informative or engaging.

Write for your audience and not your CEO.

Avoid using industry jargon and product specs in your copy. By eliminating these, you can explain the user benefits sooner.

Follow your brand standards.

Although your video is meant to engage the viewer and speak in their terms about the problems they hope to solve – it's still your video and therefore should follow your brand standards to avoid brand confusion. If you don't have brand standards...that's a story for another day.

As always, have a plan.

Before you pick up a smartphone and start recoding, have a plan. What do you want to communicate and to whom? How will you use it? What points do you want to cover? How can they best be conveyed? Is the content long enough to be spread over several videos?

Don't miss out on this valuable marketing tool. Put the power of video to work for your brand. ACTION!

CHAPTER 30

Want a Competitive Advantage? Just Ask for It.

Most businesses get their customer feedback in two ways. One is from angry, dissatisfied, or frustrated customers whose rants are rarely welcomed with an open mind or a willing ear. The other is from happy, satisfied customers whose praise we eat up with a spoon and then pat ourselves on the back with it.

While both may contain information that might prove valuable toward improving the customer experience (CX), it is the silent majority of customers that hold the key to a wealth of unmined insight that could give your business a unique advantage over your competition. Ready to mine for some of that gold? Just follow these simple tips:

Timing

Obviously, you don't want to present a customer feedback survey the instant they step into your store or visit your home page. Present the survey at the close of the transaction, whether in person or online, when the experience is fresh in their mind.

Motivation

Some businesses may offer an incentive such as a future discount or entry into a prize drawing for completing the survey. While that is nice, most customers simply want to be heard. If you position their feedback as an important and valuable tool, an added incentive may not be necessary.

Length

Not even your 83-year-old, shut-in grandmother wants to fill out your six-page survey, and she plays word search puzzles all day! Respect your customers' time and limit your questionnaire to no more than 10 questions.

Questions

Ask questions that will provide you with the greatest insight into generating greater future sales. Since your idea of what your customers might say may influence your questioning, investing in a professional consultant to help you identify the right questions is often a wise decision.

An Overlooked Opportunity

Customer feedback can be gathered in many ways. Online surveys, feedback cards (often seen in hotels and restaurants), and survey invitations printed on receipts are just a few options. But many businesses overlook the ability of employees to capture information. Train your employees to ask simple questions during the transactions such as, "Have you shopped here before?"; "Where do you usually purchase your widgets?" and, "Why did you decide to try us?", and then immediately record the responses.

Turn Data into Information

Hopefully you will get an impressive response to your survey, but don't just tally the responses so that all you have is raw data. Translate that data into information that you can use to positively impact your business.

Take Action

Once you have a clear idea of what your customers want, take action – but only if it fits your business model. You can quickly go broke trying to cater to each and every whim.

Follow up

As mentioned earlier, people just want to be heard. Follow up with your feedback participants and keep them abreast of your progress. If you've made a change they requested, they'll likely come back. If you could not honor their request, let them know that their voice was heard.

CHAPTER 31

Outsourcing Your Marketing Makes Sense

When you need a ride to the airport, do you brush the dust off your chauffeur, or do you call Uber? When you're entertaining, do you pull your chef away from the "Cupcake Wars" marathon he's been watching, or do you call a caterer? When you're ready for an adult night on the town without the kids, do you leave the kids with your au pair, or do you hire a sitter?

Unless your personal manservant is reading this to you, chances are it's the latter option for each scenario. It's called outsourcing and it makes sense. It also makes dollars and cents as you'll see below. And, what works in most homes will work for most businesses as well.

Today, a typical small business requires expertise in the following skills to successfully brand and market its services:

- Brand Strategy Development
- Copywriting
- Customer Service Measurement

- Digital Marketing
- Graphic Design
- Marketing Plan Implementation
- Media Buying
- Public Relations
- Search Engine Optimization
- Social Media Marketing
- Website Design and Development

As a business, you have four options:

1. Attempt to find someone who is an expert at all of these services and then sit back and watch his or her outrageous, although deserved, salary eat away at your profits.
2. Staff your marketing department with a diverse team of specialists who could handle your simple branding needs well before lunch – leaving them sitting idle until their next moment to shine arises.
3. Hire a marketing generalist who knows just enough to know that he or she needs outside help for certain projects and, before you know it, five different vendors are telling your brand story. Ever play the game telephone when you were a kid? Your brand messaging will likely be as consistent or effective.
4. Outsource your branding and marketing needs to a full-service agency that can be there when you need its services and off-the-clock when you don't. Let the agency absorb the cost of continuous improvement, education, subscriptions and licenses.

In addition to the expert talent, significant cost-savings, and brand consistency that come with outsourcing to a full-service agency, you also enjoy the convenience of a one-stop-shop versus multiple vendors.

As a full-service agency that functions as the outsourced marketing department for many of our clients, Electrum Branding can vouch for the effectiveness of outsourcing. Consider us the Uber of ad agencies! Just like Uber, we're:

The best way to get wherever you're going. Our goal is to help you succeed on time and under budget with a remarkable ROI.

Always on, always available. We are responsive and tend to over-communicate. You will never question the status of a project.

You rate, we listen. As customer experience (CX) measurement and management experts, we live and breathe by our service standards.

There's a ride for every price and any occasion. Monthly retainer, project-to-project, or an hourly rate – we work around what's best for you and your budget.

Ready to give your marketing a lift? Contact the branding and marketing experts at Electrum Branding and take your brand where you want it to go for a cost-effective ROI.

ABOUT THE AUTHOR

Roger D. Hicks began his advertising career in 1986 when the industry could be summed up in three words: print, TV and radio. After five years in the business, during which time he earned two Addy Awards for his copy writing and radio campaigns, Roger began his next career in the nonprofit sector.

After 15 years, he returned to his roots only to find that the world of advertising was rapidly evolving. Traditional marketing activities were dwindling while inbound marketing strategies such as blogging, search engine marketing, search engine optimization, and social media were gaining momentum.

To effectively keep Electrum Branding's clients' brands top of mind, Roger went back to school and completed his Masters Certificate in Integrated Online Marketing, making him the agency's expert in online strategies, search engine optimization and search engine marketing. And, as the demand for social media management and monitoring soared, so did his curiosity, motivating him to become a certified social media professional.

Roger is involved in every stage of every client project. When he's not managing Electrum Branding's busy production schedule, negotiating media contracts, writing copy, creating shareable online client content, or improving search engine rankings, he's forging relationships with clients. He's quick with a joke but he's faster with answers. Electrum clients know he's the "go-to" guy. His humorous, easy-going style is enjoyed by clients but what they truly appreciate is his determination to deliver results – on time and under budget.

Roger is a 33-year resident of South Florida where he lives with his husband Don and their miniature English Bull Terrier Zoe. Although a world traveler (30 countries visited so far), he is happiest at home or serving the community as a board member for the Light of the World Clinic and the March of Dimes Birth Defects Foundation.

ABOUT ELECTRUM BRANDING

We believe that great marketing comes from a strong partnership between clients and a diverse team of strategic and creative people at Electrum. So, how have we managed to create successful campaigns for our clients, time and time again, for all these years?

Evolution. Sparked by our "whatever-it-takes" mentality, the thought leaders at Electrum Branding have an incredible knack for recognizing and seizing new opportunities.

Experience. Since 2004, Electrum Branding has maintained a high level of expertise that is both deep and broad. From broadcast and billboard ads to direct mail and point-of-purchase to everything our clients need to compete in the online arena, we have a proven track record of crafting and delivering fresh, hard-hitting messages to all types of audiences. We believe that the way your team builds relationships is the best way to promote your brand, which is why we are known for "building your brand from the inside out."

Our Promise. Our turnaround times are based on agreed-upon schedules and deadlines. And, we don't miss deadlines. Period. The sun will never set without a returned phone call, email or acknowledgement from us. We believe in service standards. We're in control of our turnaround times and deadlines because we do everything in house. No excuses!

electrum
branding

Electrum Branding · 3333 West Commercial Boulevard · Suite 111 ·
Fort Lauderdale, Florida 33309 · 954.318.1600
www.electrumbranding.com

CPSIA information can be obtained
at www.ICGtesting.com
Printed in the USA
BVHW041647090321
602013BV00007B/1503

9 780578 606668